'Kate Morgan's *I
meditation on la
opening you up
and exterior. A
body. The perso
astonish. Morg
suspends reality through precision and excav...
digging deeper into experience, and also one of those
metaphysicians who finds meaning at-hand in the
daily and then disperses it all to be gathered again.
This result is potent, moving, and mysterious'

~ Nate Lippens

'It doesn't matter what genre this book is (essay,
personal diary, notebook), nor what its subject
matter is (a garden, a sculpture, the plumbing
system underlying a house, love), because in some
mysterious way, it manages to transform the
material part of the world into poetic intensity and
affect whoever holds it in their hands, as if it were
a flood, overwhelming and reassuring at the same
time. In this sense, the omnipresent water in this
truly lyrical exploration of reality seems to take over
the words and transform this text into an organism
with a life of its own.'

~ Cecilia Pavón

~~~

Kate Morgan is a writer and artist from London, living in Glasgow. Their writing has been published by Sticky Fingers, Nothing Personal, MAP Magazine, Worms, and in anthologies by Pilot Press.

~~~

INGRESS, Kate Morgan

~~~

Pilot Press,
London

~~~

I suspect that the body…might not be co-equivalent with materiality, that my body might be deeply connected to, if not be, language.

~ KATHY ACKER, *Bodies of Work*

~~~

She stands over a fish, thinking about certain irrevocable mistakes she has made today. Now the fish has been cooked, and she is alone with it.

~ LYDIA DAVIS, *The Fish*

it's all always about water ingress anyway	11
to be watertight	15
shining identification ~ not a bird, not a slug	19
select anachronica ~ via Anaïs Nin	31
to cleave liquid ~ via Roni Horn	47
bristling ~ the dehumidifier	67
afterwards ~ the rose and the lotus	79

~~~
## *it's all always about water ingress anyway*

~ You've said it before, in a kind of dramatic plumbing-related aphorism: that it all always comes down to water ingress anyway, and here, too, that was the case. It's been raining a lot, you know. To add to this, the sprinklers, whose tall stems rise up from down there, spit across in a rotary, compete with the straight down of the rain. Water is pooling where it shouldn't, out in the library courtyard. Something, not-water, is causing a blockage somewhere.

They've had four people out to look at it. The first used his bare hands, then left and returned with a short blue plunger. The others used two wooden brooms, one: the kind that's wide set and has the handle-brush joint stabilised by metal braces, the kind you can put weight into; the other: short, light, just good enough for dust, its soft bristles a side fringe by use. He lows to stroke the broom against the drain, as though it moves water. Which, it does…to a degree. This broom, despite taking a form full of gaps, does manage to put some pressure on the mass. It causes a kind of discontented wave that settles quickly back to its original shape. He urges the water and grit across the gutter, pressing hard down, guiding it where it knows to go already.

It knows the way, but there is something in the way.

Later, a new person comes out with a different plunger, a sort of turbo one. This extra-strength plunger, *'The Rothenberger,'* works. The person with the small broom still runs it across the pavingstones, moving the water away only for it to drain, draw, back, down, through. Those who are left watch the water flow down together. This passage of them watching is calm.

Their actions now become less haphazard, settling each into distinct tasks. One person demonstrates the successful method for someone else who didn't witness it, holding the turbo plunger against the tiles of the courtyard, motioning. Then, they are both brushing the space. The narrow broom skirts the edge of the building, outlines it. The wood knocks against the wall beneath the window from out of which you are watching. It knocks and goes straight through — the sound. They are brushing leaves around the courtyard, up and out of the gutter, and into a tall close arrangement, edging up to a loose stack of cement floor tiles. Someone returns and has fashioned a grid to go over the drain itself. He secures it in place and steps back. They are working together; a team, they bear the same emblems on their black polo shirts. They are wearing fresh new denim, it seems incongruous (!) but it is true. It is still an assertive blue, just yet to be dulled. This lack of use is what's incongruous. Instead of picking up the leaf pile they have made, they shift one of the cement tiles down from the stack to cover it, so it rests on a diagonal, hiding the leaves. A little habitat, maybe. *That's not going anywhere.*

Now, the next day, a different man is out there, has a bin bag with a good filling of something already — you can tell because it's standing up of its own stead. He's got gloves on and is pulling up grit and clumps of the plane trees' leaves, crudding it out with a flat painter's scraper, the kind with a side notch. He runs this, angled, along the tiles. You can hear the scrape, but not so loud as if he were over here nearer your side of the yard. He hasn't yet cleared, or even registered, that hidden pile of leaves — maybe he doesn't know.

You eat lunch out front, thinking all the time that you're missing a view on the action of that contained courtyard. You eat with S, talking. You watch someone, their head a head of bleached tight curls, with a lilac wheeled cart, enter the building. Their hues appeal. They exit a minute later loaded up with some tiles from the courtyard stack. You recognise them — they're the ones! They tip these into a new pile outside. This repeats. Then you see they've gone and bought a pressure washer, too. It is brand new. They wheel it in, up the ramp and through the entranceway. You pass it on its trolley as it waits for the lift to get up a floor. You walk. Now both up, outside again, someone lifts it out of the box, *'Titan'*, and prods their finger through the thin clear plastic. They inspect the gun part, and the tubes to which the gun might attach, coiled there near the top. Something is stiff: it doesn't readily uncoil. The person unpacking finds a cable tie that's binding it in place, and you watch as he thinks on it, pulls a chain of keys from his pocket…then reconsiders, leaves the cable tie unsnapped. Tries again with the force of a hand. Then again gets out his keys. He holds a square tag, a keychain, you can't quite make out what, palmed, as though it's the handle of a blade, with a key arrowed out from beneath his thumb and finger. He abrades this, in a sawing motion, across the cable tie. It doesn't break. He sits, then, and tries from this new angle, from this position where he needn't expend other energies, so can commit more to the motion. He manages. Still with the keys in his palm, he unspools the tube from its runners. It is a juddery thing. Now, the man who'd used his bare hands yesterday is approaching with his lunch, a filled half baguette. You look him directly in the eye. He sits, and he watches, too, as the wand gets attached to the tube…

Someone's got it working now and is adding water back into the situation. The pressure washer's been hooked up to a tap somewhere and shoots the stuff out. Your body braces for the shudder of it on the lower part of the glass wall (you know that sound travels through it like anything, like yesterday).

He has the best job, the one with the wand, the triggered wand that power-cleans — cleans so well that you can see where you've been. You can watch as the water works to lighten the floor, as the grit goes. You can draw lines of clean. Now he has his right hand, the less dominant, out flat, a straight arm supported against the sculpture (a Paolozzi, all dull grey and lateral, calm and not) and uses his left to hold the wand. He is cleaning just the base, which is a kind of cast cement, but I worry he will move on to the sculpture — get ahead of himself. The machine's essential disjunct, where a slightness of gesture controls the path of such strength, does this to you. He yields to the inclination, moves over the sculpture itself, and as it happens (!) the metal gives over its own pleasing hollow frequency. He gives it a wide stroke. He swaps hands, then switches back, steadying the barrel again. I'm sure there's a locking feature on there, but his hand remains pent up in the grip. There is an upright line between his brows.

You think about how the members of this group have set to cleaning the courtyard, how their energies have been focused here for one reason, though have now broadened to find new areas to which to commit some time, but you are more concerned with the knowledge of what *he with the pressure washer's* not realised. He started with cleaning the floor tiles, and began with a line of three, singly each. Then crossed up, did the three alongside those first three. Then later got coaxed by the form of the sculpture. Since doing that first set of six so well, he's not realised how desirable the effect of the combination of close range and a direct perpendicular angle is. He's lost that stillness that was in his face on those firsts, is using his wrist more, being flippant with it, nonchalant — he has forgotten he has the best job of them all.

~~~
to be watertight

Often there's water on her face.
You are close to her, she looks at you.

~ In Roni Horn's series *You Are The Weather*, a woman is photographed in Iceland, in different locations, lightings, weathers, in different pools of liquid. Her face is different always, like the weather is.

You read that a character in *In Search of Lost Time* says they have become *an animated barometer myself,* thinking maybe that's what this text might become, its role to be a barometer to other things: the liquid, the emotional, time.

My nana Hazel said that one only had to look at me to know what sort of day it was going to be. And that my face, mood always evident upon it, determined in a way more active than a bright sunny day, if everyone would have a good day. That I was like the weather, or the sun.

Here in Glasgow, where we are, the weather is very present, though it does not bother the text. In fact there's often an inverse relationship between the warmness of a day and the text's happening: its expansion, lengthening, sharpening, muddying. In this city the weather is both an exterior and an interior force. It affects enclosed spaces, it affects your mood; it ingresses as liquid, as coolness. It reveals difference, makes clear the temperature divide: here and out there through the window. Ingress is pulling in, soaking up, is also release. Saturate and unsaturate, entrance and exit, ingress, egress. Moisture in the air beads and sags across the inside of the window panes on cold mornings. This condensation feels uneasy, is not ingress or egress, but a *coming forward*, an *unveiling*, a pushing through to the visible. Such condensation can be described as a deviant form of ingress.

Outside, another kind of ingress: the council are at work, the uneven noise of many bodies, rakes, forks, chainsaws, as they trim the vegetation, weed the street. *Urgent gulley* and *gutter work*, said a letter. *Cleansing work*. They chop roughly, run the chainsaw flush parallel to the wooden fence. This municipal trim thinks differently to when I do it. At the doorstep thin trails grow into the porch, try and come in. I pull at them absently.

All egressions are also ingressions, all ingress is egress from some other position. To be watertight, then, is a fallacy: there is no stopping it. Things will get in. A thought, water, gets in and never really goes away. For the text, then, ingress is just that: not being watertight. It is all ingression, is a sponge, is green wood. Is changeable, flippant, and cultivates (does not prune) turns of mood and mind. This text is aware of the bodies that write it and the bodies that read it, and of how its body is different, wets differently. Changes position. By contortions of lived experience, we come to something other.

Eileen Myles says you need to say something more than once to feel it (somewhere in *Inferno, A Poet's Novel*). They say that that is how you build muscle. By holding something warm over months, you speak to and of it differently: it shines, but also slims, by handling, by dwelling. (If you shine something too much, though, it might disappear.) To restate slightly differently tells us something about language, too. It is between such aspects where the space of the text opens up, develops a thought. So, shifts in method or style get us to another vantage, and *Ingress* is a vessel for such multiples of register.

This text knows that ingress is often uncoerced.

Uninvited. That these buildings, all infrastructure, that support the forming of the text, are similar in that they, like the text, are also sponges, take in (water) without scrutiny. That the sandstone drinks up the acute rain. Liquid changes hands all the time — the points at which we meet it, then, mark time. As liquid changes hands, always moving, it changes the hands themselves too. The text *comes through* to mark this, to live in a body.

The text needs water to survive. Feels keenly the way water is coerced towards it. How it comes in indirect ways, not a straight line in from Loch Katrine. The text feels the rate of decreasing altitude, ten inches a mile, as water approaches from the loch; and feels implicitly how this is linear, narrative, even though that's only six and a half metres of a drop in total from there to here. The text knows that water knows it must flow downstream, as the text knows that its own end will be after its beginning. This text bristles for ingress all the time, and is an attempt to satisfy and interpret this state of being.

~~~

shining identification ~ not a bird, not a slug

I

~ The turn of autumn. I watch the progress of the dog roses in the paths near Shields Road, down by the side of the motorway, where there used to be a canal. Smell the flimsy-wrinkle petals, the strength of scent! But really I'm here for what's under, those rounding green packages, those warm hips, at the base of each. They widen daily. I am waiting for them to blush red. Even in midsummer I looked at the rosebuds with some disdain, OR — a vampyric interest largely in their fruits and not their flower.

Another day I go East looking for them, to less avail. On the way home, sodden, I pass a bush of lavender, run my hands over the stems as though rubbing shampoo into someone's hair. Palms to face to smell. On the next corner, as I turn into the end of my street, a man stands all in white, trousers hitched up to above his knees, bare-legged in the centre of a newly formed lake. Cars reverse, change direction, when they see it up ahead. In clean fast arcs on the wet tarmac they go to take some other route. It's been raining hard for hours, the drains have had their fill or are blocked, can take no more. He is holding a rake, maybe. I can't see the end of it. The street has in a series of proximate instances become brimming precipice, all welling all welling up.

Wells might fill in this sort of rain. Floods might flash, moors sponge up, their shoulders heaving with it. And, tears well as water wells in wells, roundly and voluptuously, about an edge. I let them when they come, which D says is often and openly. When they say this I think at first that they speak of my aptness to cry as a kind of greenness in the negative: a childish thing to do, something that the wise, the woody, don't. (Remember, I am but green wood.) But really it's a clearing, a necessary and good flushing, an ardence, a self at the fore.

This brimming — of liquid, of trees on the cusp of fruiting, of roses on the edge of hipping, of emotion on a face — this brimming shows what is *to come*. Jamaica Kincaid ends *Earthly Delights* on these words: *An integral part of a gardener's personality — indeed, a substantial amount of a gardener's world — is made up of the sentiment expressed by the two words 'To Come'.* People talk about pregnant pauses, they love to use this phrase, for its alliterative brim — and, is every garden this? Each leaf a pause pregnant with *what will be*, those *to comes*, and even at something's peak, holding fast to the knowledge of its passing.

Some plants, and I am thinking really of camellias, give us a constance of green, are evergreen, a steady, daily, shoe-shine green that knows its brilliance. As a camelia's buds set, seem to both tighten and enlarge, each suggests a warm future shade of petal. They flower, and are of least interest in their blooming. I feel active dismay. But — I go to them with rapture when they are flagging, especially those mature ones up the hill, over West, where they flag in number, soiling in unison, dozens of faces of flowers remarking openly as to their state, as tears. I feel I cannot stare at them too long: I'm too akin, too abrim. Then, a long pause of days before they drop in noiseless thuds. Soft, turned over, they stud the pavement. Cold, soggy, cold compresses. Their crude ending brings me closer to them.

Neither the idea of their ending, nor the peak of flowering are my focus: the turn is. The turn of the globe about a day, the turn of the globe about the sun. How the turn is where the drama is, how to notice events unfolding is itself an act of intimacy. Sara Ahmed speaks of how Lauren Berlant taught her to *notice an unfolding as a way of holding something, lightly*, and I think that you can do this with a garden, and with a text. You can cling to it or you can hold it in an open hand of fingers — acknowledge its state and set it back down. Maybe do something, but more to see what follows than to alter it in a hard way.

Turns of the self are metered by implicit knowledge, like the comfort of a bud, but also like the steadying aloe coolant that greenness offers in the face of ends. All's pivoting pivoting, untwisting twisting twisting. There is no end.

The magnolia by the front step is all green, the leaves in weeks will turn to bright-lit candles, to orange. The buds for flowers next year, by which time the leaves will have dropped to just the mantle, the candelabra, of branches, have already set. They are robed in fur to get through this time, 'til it is warm enough come early spring, when they will open to white, cream, urging to pink, blooms on this leafless tree. It is these buds, though, now, October, that are the current burgeoning, that show the brim. In preparing themselves, they are noticing the precipice, then. This looking forward flexes the boundary of each thing. A person, a seed. You run into A on the street, speak a second, and she knows you are abrim. Watch a snapped branch flagging in the same breath, and something nearby—

>is green, green, greener than before,
>eating up the sunlight.
>sated and full of the green. Until…

...here, in this garden,
One day, digging, I found a bone.

Digging, sorting, redistributing different kinds of earth. Clodding it all into a tub and shaking so that the light stuff rises. One day, digging, I found a bone. Don't look too hard, set it aside on a protruding corner somewhere. Think little of it, maybe a cat's skull — but really it's obvious: a single vertebra. This is confirmed by C, stressed at its handling. The next day, set it out and take a photograph, a straight index finger held beside it for scale. A message comes back with a conclusion of *a small or juvenile fox or cat*. That *small or juvenile* tickles a nerve. Neither of its two possible options leaves me unfeeling.

Why might a young fox die? I asked of some websites. They come up with a range of hypotheses,

one:
They are born without sight, so, for the first weeks of their lives, before sight comes, they are more vulnerable to predators, who will skulk around waiting for their parents to go off.

two:
Sometimes foxes kill their young, the male *dog foxes*, in order to keep down competition, OR they kill the young of other foxes, in order to avoid the necessity of adoption when a parent has died.

The dog foxes will be newly born by Easter, the dog roses will be in bloom and scent in midsummer: with this you can count a year.

II

~ It is September: the weather is pressing, the scent of hops brooms across the city from the breweries in the East, the sweet peas are frailing with the rainfall and a general tiring of the season. Berries on trees begin to show. The rowan's: a plastic yellow-orange. They just appear, theatric, you've no sense of long burgeoning as you do with the hips.

In Glasgow my garden grows, a lovely *L* around the tenement block. And, this garden is bound to another, to Hazel's, whose shape was like a scarab. The garden surrounded her house, which clung softly to a slope, so most of the upper floor was also at a level with the ground. Because of this, she lived in continual relation to the outside: the green always looking into the rooms. Sleeping then at ground level, looking out at dawn you might see deer at rest on the lawn. They recognise you, flicker, depart. Her last summer, from that same room, she asked me to move one of the plants, out from its pot and into one of the lower, steeper bits near the greenhouse. It was something like an aeonium, with pale pastel leaves, and the midsummer soil was shaggy dry around its root ball when I took it out of the earth. She described the spot she wanted it to go in with words, from her bed. I did this for her, then told her I had. Even then she was still maintaining her environment, the house, the garden: during that period I also relined the curtains in the lounge at her instruction, a gesture carried out in a difficult preemptive knowledge that she wouldn't see them bleached over by sun again.

Her gone, we had to leave her garden, so I uprooted that same aeonium again and took it with me. It had her matte claggy clay soil all around its base still, this time moist with September. Over a few years and several flats, it stayed in a pot, and by the time I found a way to this garden, to this home, I knew it was nearing death. I planted it in this almost death in mid-December, out at the base of the lounge window, so it would die into the soil here, its nutrients with it. Planted it to die.

That seemed important, a kind of iteration, an anointing. Meaning, her garden is here, in material and also in mind. Because our relationship was borne out in her garden, the mindframe I come to garden with is always lit by hers, though shaded by our difference. Where her sense of self, security and identity were stable, mine's always been fluid, constant only by discomfort, by the feeling of alterity in enough contexts. This is such that I'm wont to think of relation, of difference, in the garden, where she wouldn't think to think like that at all. She saw me as the sun, as something *as* bright, watching my face for shifts in heart and mind. And I felt a different being to her. Me: my thinking self, my body, and this queer, optic way of noticing, of siting myself at removes. In her garden, I knew my body as alien within the space — as not a plant. I took comfort in this outright difference, being so cut and dry, so sure and clean, not at all like my relationship to girlhood.

There's a part in Robert Glück's *Margery Kempe* where a garden is described. There, *flowers and birds shone with individual life and identification with their species, an elaborate and finicky charm*. I am seeking something near this: I look to *shiningly identify*. To what, I don't know.

In *Margery Kempe*, specific elements held close to historical accuracy. Like the birds — their calls, their number, their shape and colouring — all were true to place and time. All had this: their own shining identification. In the book, true specific birdsong is held against other things that are less verifiable: all subjectivity and the telling of stories, fantasies, sex. The security and distinctness of such verifiables as the birds has the effect of lighting every thing Glück touches with the sense of it as something truly having had occurred — moments are lit up as true, given a buffed new sheen by the birds. Beside one another, opposing, these objective and subjective elements have the effect of offering *each other* shining identification; they mark as truth the touch of a hand on a leg, tears welling, and TOO as lived truth the song of a bird on that day, its angled leg.

When I think of a bird in a garden shining with such *elaborate finicky*-ness, such specificity, I do not know if that bird knows its specificity by difference, by comparison with other species, or by similarity, by commune with its own. Perhaps though there is a third option: that a bird's shining is an internal quality unreliant on an observing other. A bird that *shone*, as in Glück's formation, requires an observing body, whereas something that is *shining*, the word I am drawn to use, is shining of its own volition. There might be nothing else other than its shining; there is no need for a dialogic encounter. I am not there yet; I am not a bird; I don't have it in me.

If shining identification is to come from within, then perhaps these subjectivities, fantasies, an imagined (or real) human hand on a human leg, are its catalyst. If, as Glück says, *a story reveals the body in order to verify its existence*, I could similarly look to other things to verify my own shining, to verify my existence. I want to ask — can a shining body be its own observer? Because, there is a core difference between shining and reflection. Shining is light without image. Shining can be a shared state, is more sensual than an image. Reflection is image and light and surface all at once. One's own shining, though, can only be known via an internal, mutual system of reflection: buttercups on chins, surfaces close but not touching, light and room in between. Shining is made up of light, ardent, excessive. Controlled attendance to oneself or another, burnishes, then might burn.

III

~ I'm with Hazel in her kitchen making lunch. It's summer and I am tall enough to be looking down on the counter. On it, the breadboard, and beside that a knife with a broad blade and a white handle. Beside that — a wasp! I let her know. There it was, on the counter, beside the breadboard, beside the knife. She came over and, as though it were the most natural thing, without thought or anxiety, took up just the handle of the knife, the blade-tip staying in touch with the counter, and twisted it a hundred and eighty degrees, so that the blade was now, again, flush with the counter, the wasp held in between and crushed, dying, dead. I loved her guile, her calm. I was shocked, lit up, elated with the brutality and the peace of it. Later, years later, a hive bedded itself into a wooden bit on the side of her house, quite near this site of death, and hundreds of wasps circulated in every downstairs room.

Was nature there *in bonds*? Hazel saw death as necessary. Sometimes this meant killing things by her own hand, but also it meant not worrying over death when it did happen: if plants died or a cutting didn't take, or things became enfeebled in the greenhouse from a harsh frost, she was not fazed. This was strength — holding greenness, its trial and power, but also holding the knowledge of its finitude, its frailing limits. I want to attribute to ardence a kind of concentration, a burning, fixed attention, sometimes too earnest. Like a burning glass, *verre ardent*, that concentrates light and focuses it on a specific thing to inflame — to pull liquid from, away, a burning intensive parching. You look away.

What does it mean to live close to death in this way? To be thrilled but also metered by it. In *Modern Nature* Jarman talks regularly about destruction, especially the way in which the weather so affected his chosen site at Prospect Cottage. He buys plants often: lots of them don't take, die. He states this perfunctorily in his diary. He buys more, gathers seeds from the annuals. I take this to mean there has to be ardence at the offset, a trust that something might happen — that a seed might grow; but also a kind of fatalism — that very often it won't.

Was Derek Jarman green? Yes. Near the end of the film *The Garden*, he closes a book and gets up from his Androniack chair. He's goofy, charming, *green*. Then, the chair, or at least *a chair*, is burning on the beach. Is greenness intractable from the edge of its faltering? From death? Is there bound up in it the point at which it will be green no longer? When he came up to Glasgow in the autumn of 1989, Jarman described a city where *Inky black clouds looming over charcoal temples smudge china blue skies*. He searched about for things to burn, to cover in pitch and feathers under railway arches. There's the destructive and the constructive, in the same way that to make a garden, utopic, also incurs destruction. Do I use the garden as a place where I can verify my presence, where I can effect change and then see the results over time, and might that simplistic quid pro quo be very green of me? In this garden, my *L*, each of my interventions sum to few. I try and let go, because points where I have forged through and made clear marks on the space come to seem ghastly...

I cut back the hedge and am left with a pile of stems. They sit for weeks, like a Nash painting, but without the order that comes with distance and with depiction. The stems leftover (still living) look bedraggled, unevenly shorn, *y* upon *y* of branches, splitting off, up up up then an end. Few leaves remain. It makes me exposed: it is like the seafront out here, now, instead of a private green corridor. The morning after I'd gone out for air; it was cold, white, windy, a hinting drizzle, and I thought *I have made a grave error*.

Eventually one day I sorted the stems, put the smallest into a container, picked out from them a lime green caterpillar and placed it gently, ardently, on the arm of the bench. Exposed. A minute later it had disappeared. I watched the robin, long of leg, hop down the path away from me, some curved line in its mouth?

...

March: a crocus hanging on, the hyacinth almost, the peony just dark pink metallic thumbs pricking up through the soil. This piece of writing has been a thorn since I began writing it, so for almost a year probably. *Now, two years*. It is March again and the foxcubs will be being born, and I don't know what to say of them. But, there is something in here, something about the letting go of expectation, something fatalistic. That lots of things won't work. That, once you're monitoring and have tried to force the things into a context as close to a lab as possible, you're not really gardening anymore. There's something about being okay when something dies. Metering in order to be able to continue. There's lots about feelings of alienation, which are felt in the garden, but more keenly felt in other places. I'm listening to McKenzie Wark talking to hannah baer about techno, and maybe this is what the garden is for me: *My theory about techno is that it's not really made for humans at all [...] techno is not really made for any body at all, so I feel equally as alienated as anybody else in it, therefore I feel at home*. A garden's made in part by humans, but that doesn't mean it's made for them, the multiples of difference it holds is a comfort. I know myself as alien here. As so much larger than the rest of them, but the trees. Alien to the strawberries, to the hedge, to the slugs and the gravel, even. I know myself as alien, but as an alien among aliens. Slugs have sex in rounds, together make the shape of sweet cardamom buns atop the morning grass. In that relation I am outwith: I am not a slug, I bed on a mattress, not the earth.

Later, it's night and you're in the garden to put something in the compost bin. Secure the lid, glance up. A lamp is on in the lounge and you see what the garden sees: the room a lantern amidst the black. The garden is witness to the house, as at Hazel's, and the inhabitants of the garden face an interior tableau such as this nightly.

~~~
select anachronica ~ via Anaïs Nin

I

You sit on the step, in the sun,
and you spill your coffee, apologise.
Their eyes are shut to the heat the warm,
they say *don't worry, it's your loss, none got on me.*
Their socks are dry still.
The coffee stain runs clean the following day
with the rain.

All the above are facts, true blobs that record events that happened in that sequence. They are listed facts, chronological. Yet — the fact is only fact in the action of its moment. After its moment, it is just a truth that was true at a certain time,

and that time is in the past.

The oldest fact is the first: *you sit on the step, in the sun*, and it prevails for most of the sequence. But —
in time, becomes false in a number of ways:

    with bodies moving,
    with weather being what it is,
    with *you* peeling into you and me.

    Them and you.

In the days that follow, when you're separately alone both truth and fact begin to ellipse...all these true blobs of your time together, you and them, concur to something other. Later still, when they try to write, happened things try to get committed to language and what *was present* can only be written about as they are encountering it pressing into the past. This pressure is also a funnelling, a snorkelled heightened thing.

Deeper still, the slick of a moment pours away, from you, from itself.

You can write the past, and you can write the future, but you cannot write the present.

(Mette Edvardsen)

> Can you write in the mind while an action is going on, though?
> Can those two fingertips, a feeling and words for it, touch in unison?
> Can a phrase, an act, be tongued and written in synchronicity?

— And, can you even spell it right
if
we are living in another world?
if
*our having bodies is a farce,
an anachronism?*

(Anaïs Nin *Under a Glass Bell*)

You wonder how to use their body,
how to carry it, how to enact it,
if they believe that its very being is a farce — a lie,
and a lie too that is anachronistic: that's out of time.

> You injure yourself
> send them photos of the scrapes on your
> shoulder and side
> and these are as explicit—
> Your body is open to the cold of your room,
> they can feel the cold.

What is anachronic is that their body's presence exceeds the time you are together, that they do feel this cold, from distance, and from the vantage too, of hours later. Anachronism is things off-kilter, maybe an offsetting, OR — two bodies running parallel but not to the same metre because your metre is not their metre because

> time is convulsed.
> Out of time with itself,
> it knows neither of its elbows.

They realise that for minutes, longer, they've been thinking of your mouth's volume as two times, three times, their own. A being whose actions seem anachronistic (they think the word), that alters its location. This is not a mouth but some extra-worldly vehicle, this smudges over, this moves freely, refocuses, escalates. Spatially a kind of ship.

Later, they ask if you've thought about Wednesday, and you have, but — only of the way they acted, how they stood on the top of your feet, not

    of words spoken.

    Of pressure,
    of the pads of each of their toes,
    of the weight of their two heels against the tops of
    your toes.

Now, unspeaking across a table, sharing alone a line between two eyes, two eyes, you both think about that Wednesday. That day widens into the space of this day, a moment, a beat. Its cadence lifts, lengthens…you paste Wednesday into the now, recur it again again,

'til, you both have *the cadence of a bulb flowering*,
that cadence that is applied to the memory of the thing,
that cadence that exists in the whelk of the silence between you.

As hindthought repeats each statement (silent), each action (static), they become stamen, flossy with pollen… and maybe all that the anachronism is is that you are *both* in another world, different from the one you seem to be in, but one in common.

We are living in another world.

It's still day. Time presses into you through the front door. Your anachrony meets the chronic daylight. You are out of sorts with chronos, god of time. In disagreement about what is time. Unfeigned by their metrics, not just out of sync with time, but outwith it altogether: antagonists to the notion of it all. You do not know if you and they tried to time any thing you'd get it right. No thing can be itemised or peeled-from to a human minute, because each is happening at once, unfielded:

together and apart.

Words got down to show total surface brittleness, where temporal material tenderness, from object to object, matter to matter, to body, to matter, to object's all flung up — and keenly recognised: the lukewarm coffee's uneven spill and quickening cool against the sun-heated stone step, each changing each's surface qualities. Then the pleasure of the way the rain, usually so aloof in matters of people, thought to intervene, washed these evidences clear away. Things (rain, stone, a cuff) are desirous, contain the momentum of agency, seek to kiss in their own ways. Somewhere, they read that the lamp whose oil drips and burns the sleeping cupid, waking them, *wanted to "touch so lovely a body – to kiss it in a lamp's way."* ('The Golden Ass,' quoted in Susan Griffin *Pornography and Silence*)

A lamp-kiss is contact.

The light of the lamp kisses you, the handle of the nice knife as you slice kisses you, the floorboards kiss your soles singly and in pairs. You move across them. The chair in which you sit kisses you, returns a little of your pressure on it back. The sheets kiss at their corners. They are dry from hanging, can feel their own crisp salinity. You kiss the sheets together as you fold them, in half, in half, in half again, each becoming a loose even self-contained thing, not flighting like an open sheet. Stacked in the chest, these folded kisses are longer, more intentional.

A lamp-kiss is pressing.

Night, too, presses, gloaming. You are in the kitchen together. You read from their cabinet, in their hand, a list of words to describe the ideas that might fill this body of writing. They've written, in phthalo green, *Pressing Weight*, then added, in pencil, + *specificity*.

You ask for this.

— might contact, then, pressing, be a form of anachrony? A counter to time that holds the farce of their bodies? When time (or anything else) is pressing, it means imminence, which is maybe as close to being in-time-with as we can get. Closer than a clock. An assurance of a tied reality, even if it isn't this one.

You survey their belly like it's a plate of pasta,
maybe shells,
where you can singly pick but where each bite is ostensibly the same.
Picking judiciously what bit to kiss with
a concentration unnecessary.
You attends to this,
your face serious, thinking.

Is contact the only measure of time we can rely on?

Our having bodies is a farce.

We are living in another world.

II

You spill a jug of water.
It's sturdy
so doesn't break,
but the water pools
against the floorboards, just visible by glints
in the dim light.

You leave the room,
they think of you thinking in the bathroom,
selecting a small towel from the small pile.

You come back,
hold it up to check it's appropriate:
they assent.

Now, you've taken off your socks and are walking
the towel into the puddle,
walking the puddle into the towel.
They remove a single sock and try and do the same.

Their thinking of your thinking here is more rapt than your own moments of thought on the same subject, and is this anachrony? — that those seconds are longer for them than for you lived. That they bring *the cadence of a bulb flowering* to actions such as these (Anaïs Nin *The Labyrinth*). That the specificity of knowing a thought is happening in time in place in another self (not linguistic, abstract), is so delicious to them. For pressure from the room they're in to thin: to move instead along along down the hall, into and against the towel-room. And why should they bring this slow cadence? This bulb-flowering lighting to all? And why should they think longer on it past the date? And why should they have such deciduous fantasies as the choosing of a towel?

All these thought-actions are anachronic, and too, antagonistically futile. This is their luxury. This is your luxury. That flippant things become large, that the minor can be what they spend their time on. Their work is the work of the word, not of the body any longer. Their body is the *external envelope* that mobilises the work. The body serves the work of the word, though, needs to be fed, needs to carry out an action to see its fit, needs to lean against surfaces and try them for timbre.

In the daytime and early evening, to work, they wear a corduroy house coat over their clothes. It is cotton, quite cobalt blue, and quilted on the inner, with the fine vertical cord on the outer. Though it wouldn't do in the rain, it is a kind of overcoat. Worn with age, with the wear of an unknown body. In outline the shape of a hill in a picture book, a soft handwritten lilting *n*. It has buckles across, each the shape of the character of the word *clasp*: precise, metallic, useful, they have a pleasing snap to open and to close. These link into little brass *Ds* on the other side of the envelope. When it's done up with a body between it, the quilted face on the inner of one kisses the corduroy face on the outer of the other. Together they overlap: a lapping joint. Four of these laps build to a single continuous lap, down from their chin to their hips.

This fabric kiss warms their body, it warms the fabric too. They absently flick open and closed a clasp as they write. You do not see this action, you do not see them at work, you do not know this coat. They try and rive a gap between work-time and the time they give to you, though the mind continues. You sleep, while they spend all dreams thinking there is work to be done. That there is object upon object that needs sorting in the bedvessel. That amongst all the sheets are items that need itemised. They turn to face you and the blanket's all bunched up, a full paragraph or a full list of words. Each of these unsorted objects has important specificity, relates differently to those around it, needs to go in a considered location. But, the knowledge of any specialty, any descriptive word at all, is gone by daylight. Time presses into you through the front door. When you close the bed they are surprised by the flatness, there are no objects below its surface. Their anachrony meets the chronic daytime.

Another time, you ask, *do you have a jumper*. None of your questions end in question marks.

You wear their Guernsey, it hugs your arms where it drinks their whole half. They tell you how it's specific to that island (false), and about the way it's knitted,

> how it has
> this drop shoulder,
> how it has
> this wide neck.

> Vertical lines of knit count up
> and down and around
> your neck.

They tell you *you've got it on inside-out and backwards,*

> your head disappears.
> Unfurl it from itself,
> put it back on.
> You roll back the cuffs a touch, they watch.

A story reveals the body in order to verify its existence.
                    (Robert Glück, *My Community*)

After you leave, they look to see if there are any marks over them, if there's any legible utterance of you, any half-linguistic fallout. No — no inscriptions, impressions, half-circles, reverbs occur that quote you. You wore the Guernsey but it only verified your existence to them for the time in which you wore it: as a body coming through, as something breathing whose breaths spread out the grain of the knit, that put it under pressure, whose arms made arms out of two dimensions. When your head disappeared it did not exist.

The next time you see them they'll tell you how they've read now that you can, you should, wear it backwards, wear it all the ways, that its design is so that your arms don't wear it too much all in one place. To even the impression that a body makes, that your body makes. When they wear it after they think about the way it encompassed your arms: how they could see them through it. They instead are swamped by the wool, their self becomes just shoulder tips holding two top corners, then two wrists, two hands out the cuffs.

They read from Nin:
...I have no body. I have an external envelope which deludes others into thinking I am alive.

They spend time when they're alone thinking about this external envelope. They observe it in reflective surfaces, watch it under the bathwater, for how it bends light. Differently, when they're not alone they're more frank about it, use it more as an agent rather than for its material qualities. You tell them its material quality, though, in tongued words, in feedback loops. You hold me.

Yes, they are envelopes that embrace other envelopes, but *I have no body.*

III

They are cleaning the back of their leather sofa with diluted dettol in a spray bottle and a blue j-cloth. The back is made up of square panels strung against the wooden frame and sewn together on the vertical, making a row of three. They wipe the damp cloth across these seams. The leather is taut, but for at one seam where it's opened to a gap. The sofa is the same age as them: 27. You text. The coffee's on the hob in the other room, they just remember. It's overheating, steaming with the pressure. They run down the corridor to catch it, and as they do they hear the pangs of their phone in the dark as the message comes through. They leave it, think *I'll work for twenty minutes and then save you for after*. Put the milk on the flame, low, to warm, go back to cleaning the cushions in the sun. Just at the window, the rain has beaded in prim rounds against the smoke tree's leaves.

They sit like Kathy did, cross-legged, with just the keyboard pressing into their lap, back upright, bones of their bum into the floor, they read your message, it's quite benign. Often, they'll pitch things outwards, in your direction — like, on the train: *I sank into a labyrinth of silence […] I would not even sigh* (from Nin, *Under a Glass Bell*) — but you don't catch them. This is okay, is also your anachrony.

zigzagback

A story reveals the body in order to verify its existence,
yet it's an incomplete revelation;
we fall into the mystery, then return.

(Glück, *My Community*)

Coffee ready, in the kitchen, I have my phone on its side and propped up against the pepper mill. How to get someone to want to be slow in the writing? Inside the writing — in its reading. A reading that's like what the writing felt like. To want to stay in it and not to rush through it, to not be looking for ends, peaks: in the writing, in the reading, in your interactions. To be aware of its anachrony, and to relate to it in this mode. Anachrony as a mode of resistance. To do what you desire in any discrete moment, not thinking further along, be it seconds hours minutes days, ahead.

I have my phone like this and am drinking the milky coffee. On it plays the video of Kathy Acker at the ICA (she feels in a hurry, has just said she's worried about time). I pause it, to give her more time. There's a smudge of something on the table that's dried dark, a warm shade of green black. You scratch at it, absent. K is waiting to speak.

The keyboard's again in my lap, and I can just make out these words on the screen further down the table as they get scribed in its aether. The phone screen has gone dark, I forgot it, and then it vibrates: one, jarring, rough nudge against the metal of the pepper mill. The ridge-gap of space between the back of the phone and the mill, and the fact of it standing on its side edge, a resting torso, makes this vibration all the more linear. There's no soft surface to muffle it, it's all jawbone, hipbone, the table, the glass of water, the water in it moving with the motion of my typing, the plate, the spoon, the broken up flapjack, the cooling coffee in its cup. On the phone, they press both elbows into the fronts of your shoulders.

As I type about this vibration, another text comes through and I feel it again, that rattle. It's hermes, the messenger god: four pieces of clothing have arrived at the corner shop. To leave a hot cooling coffee to nip out to get them? To try them on? To allow another day to be lost to thinking of fabric, of the body in fabric, of a novel boundary between them? To think how they might encompass them? To leave a hot cooling coffee?

I do. I try them on, pick two to keep, then directly pack up the others and walk back over to the shop to return them. If the person working at the shop was looking for *the cadence of a bulb flowering*, they might think of what this act of swift return means. How it means a discrete knowledge of a window of time in which a body was enfolded in those items, re-wrapped and passed across the counter. This possibility, the maybe-thought in them, and your thinking of the maybe-thought: both are delicious to you. It's not the same as returning them a day later, where no time of wear can be pinned to minutes, where the clothes will be back to room temperature. No, it's not the same as the clear knowledge of most of what a stranger's been doing for the last twenty minutes — removing items of clothing, putting on others, observing how these hold their body in a mirror, how different cloths hold differently, then re-dressing in the same clothes as before. A body deciding which clothes might be permitted to hold them again, and which to return to you. No, it's not the same.

The whelk here is *because* of time, because of its specificity, because it enfolds intimacy if you can filter it to a small enough drop, if you can wrangle it so. You choosing a towel in the other room, them putting their body into clothes two doors down from the corner shop. It's a mode of resistance to be actively anachronic, there's an erotics to it, and sometimes this means just not being where you are in time, being in the room or the building across from you, being in another world. You putting your body into clothes, them choosing a towel in the other room, you spilling your coffee.

~~~
to cleave liquid ~ via Roni Horn

I   *water*

~ M recommends Roni Horn's ideas about anhydrogyne to you: a portmanteau of hydra (water) and androgyne (itself andras man, and gune woman), all from the Greek. So: man-water-woman. (Later you try to find Horn saying this word, but can't. The seed is planted, though, even though it might be a false one.) You say that she was an artist you revered as a teenager, for all the footnotes in *Still Water (The River Thames, for Example)*, for all the, what felt like, spilling intelligence. Later, alone, you think about what it would have meant to you then, to actually think about Horn: about her way of being a woman, you, stuck in a school where an idea of a shared female identity was what had corralled all those people into that place, ladies, girls. You think about how you didn't focus at all on the artists themselves, then, just on their practices. How you tried to scalpel them away from their work, or didn't even bother to watch them talk, or see how they presented, to project your life forward at all.

Within a quarter of an hour of M and the others leaving, speaking as they left of what great (dry) weather Scotland had given them, and of the assurances that every local gave, that they *really were* lucky, the kitchen darkened perceptibly. Rain fell, gushing from somewhere. A bucket upturning, over, over, down, down. You go to shut the storm door. Water is almost pooling on the black and white tiles in the porch, your shoes and recycling have been sprayed by the not-vertical rain. You watch it a moment. The front step is heady with the lemon geraniums, who've, at the touch of water, given up their scent. It is lifted off: airborne by rainfall.

Then, you spend all weekend, floodlit in the front room by the windows on two sides (South and West), watching the rain gut the sky, hearing that violence, and listening to Horn speak. You watch a conversation between her and a curator at LACMA, and her words percolate. You annotate them, they you; they filter in and permeate the room. The rain continues to gut the sky of itself. In a lapse of it, you walk down the road to the cobbler, whose shop is in the doorway of a Morrison's. Where you are it's dry, but you see a flossy line of rain falling over to the South, lit by full sun. You stop, look.

The week ends, and then renews, a few times. So, *an/hydrogyne* might not be something Roni Horn said. You still can't find it anywhere. *Anhydrogne*, a water between gender, a liquid in the middle. She *says*:

> *Of course water is the master of liquid but glass is not far behind.*

Horn says this *of course* midway through the conversation and it jars. The phrase goes unchallenged, as though it's a given truth that *water is the master of liquid*. She is saying how glass is in a liquid state all the time: how it is not a solid, how it just appears so. And how too this gives her *access to the liquid identity*.

There is watery auld glass in the windows here,
in Glasgow.
You see it sometimes, passing by.
Antique glass that didn't hide so much as the stuff we've now.

Glass that doesn't try to look like it's not there at all,
that alters the surface of things on its other side,
that catches light and doesn't just let it pass through
unquestioned.

You watch for it as you walk by, for those swift moments
where light catches its wobbly surface. You half stop—

>   *of course water is the master of liquid but glass is not
>   far behind.*

Glass hurries to catch up with you to say *I know you*.

She says it again (you rewatch the video). Flippantly, unchallenged, it insinuates itself into the dialogue — like it's really a given, like *water is wet* or *night is dark*. Such elemental thinking, and elemental material enquiries, are a crux to Horn's output, in her practice (sculpture, writing, drawings, photographs) and in her candid speaking on it. The statement shocks you, the kind of steady jarring that must contain a truth. It sinks in, sinks somewhere. You repeat it aloud to yourself, lowering into a hot bath, and then into all baths hence.

There was a point last year where you noticed that your body left a layer of a kind of silt after emptying the bath of its bathwater. Grit of different weights and shades, you had to use the shower head to rinse it down the plughole. You noticed it but didn't exteriorise the noticing into words, neither to yourself nor to others. Rather, you took tacitly this to mean that your own body had begun to secrete this sort of silt, like you'd finally turned to stone and this was just the dust that inevitably forms at the bottom of a bag, a sack, a pile of rocks. I am a pile of dry rock and this has come from me, you thought.

Horn goes on:
>   *glass… is uh technically a supercooled liquid*
>
>   *even though in part of its life it has that illusion
>   [of solidity]… uh,*
>
>   *it is in fact liquid, and at room temperature
>   appears [she emphasises the word]
>   to be solid*

You are hassled, thinking of this illusion, of what the edge between what one is and what one appears as might look like, of how to access the meeting rim of those different states. You think: this is like the system of a tent, where the inner lining makes contact with the outer lining at some time during the night, usually by cause of bodies moving, wakeful, slumbering, voluntary, involuntary…

                                     and water just comes right through.

    Funny — that a structure designed in essence as shelter, in essence to keep water at bay, can be scuppered by so human a flaw as contact, by not everything maintaining its position in stasis for any good length of time. Polyester on polyester, ingress occurs by such fingertip contact, cheek on cheek, a momentary grazing of a lip of fabric over the cheek of another that then becomes stuck, held, by this transmission.

    Held by their act of communication, distinct separate panels communicate water. They communicate (pass, share, tell) water over a membrane. Put another way — they communicate water across their two semi-permeable membranes by virtue of their shared contact. Two oppositions make their inverse. You like that something that's waterproof can fault in this way, by contact, that two of something counter one another, a polyester double negative.

You think: communication of liquids is exacerbated by contact. Two like fabrics overlap, create a kind of moiré effect, where instead of a doubled barrier — creating even less permeability, and more steadfastness of the fabric — they act in unison, match and chime. Two fabrics make a concert. This concert allows

> the two weaves of fabric to line up,
> line up, lock
> in a moment, to create a more easy chute
> a syphon route,
> a path not a boundary,
> an agreement of access:
> a yes.

A *yes* and water is communicated, comes right through.

> *so that's what's going on there...* (Roni again)

A *moiré*, from the french, *watered*, is the pattern that you discover for yourself when you put two pairs of tights on at once, for school, in the colder months, where the grid of one pair upset, reset, the optics of the grid of the second pair, and this wavy floop happened, on your legs at seven o'clock, still dark outside, getting ready. The scent of a fresh September multipack of tights is still something that takes you the whole way back to that place, to that age and to that sickly feeling. Then on your legs at eight o'clock, waiting and not wanting to get in through the school gates.

and one of the kind of virtues of that fact is that it gives me access to the liquid identity.

In the night the tent sucks together its surfaces, the inner and the outer. Water crosses over. To measure the water penetration quotient of any given fabric you need to measure its hydrostatic head, HH. This is the pressure of water that can be applied to a section of fabric before liquid passes through its surface. It is measured using a machine that applies a column of an increasing volume of liquid to a surface. Then droplets appear, water just comes right through, delicious, burgeoning, ripe spheres, through the weave. Here is the point at which a measure is taken, this the metric of waterproofness of the fabric, *say 2000 HH*.

As water breaks through, this allied tent skin forms an alley, an aqueduct across a millimetre, a provisional communicating artery. Aqueducts were built to communicate water from place to place. A viaduct communicates a person or vehicle from place to place. Sometimes they appear similar, or double up, AND — you didn't know that that bridge up towards Maryhill, which always did seem to be breaching water as you walked under it, actually carries the canal, and that all canals are aqueducts, though often their main purpose might be other than the movement of water. More like: the aqueous passage of people or goods from place to place.

Aqueous — in, or by means of, water.

Aqueducts were built by humans — artificiality is crucial to them, as gardens. Aqueducts require gravity. They hold the weight of water, and too use this quality in order to transport it, this way, that way. They are temporary vessels — water is always changing hands. Egressing, ingressing, it moves through them, across them, over them, via them. Aqueducts are feats of engineering that signify control over a landscape, the harness of resources — of liquid — by gravity.

In September you go to Greenock, not to see the sea but to see the aqueduct there: 'Main Aqueduct'. To walk alongside it and get a feel of its wetness, its mass, its length.

Early, the aqueduct was just a fine clear stream, with chunky bridges over it like slices of bread. Chamfered turf edges on those brown bread bridges.

Rose to a mist all over, a liquid density that obscured our wider surroundings. It lit the cobwebs — you could see it moving across as the sun started to warm the air and disperse it, a moist breeze made visible.

Points or areas of filtration…of boundaries between the human, cut and forged routes for the water, and these mossy edges, their lines broken like more pieces of bread with hands.

> *flume* - An old term for a wooden or metal box channel : an aqueduct.
> *gate* - In a sluice or canal, a structure of vertical sliding boards or metal that controls the flow of water (as in a "watergate").

After the point of midday, a fast waterfall. Sitting at its base, soggy underfoot, high grass and dappled evaporation, out of most of the heat of the day's sun. At later points, from sitting and from standing, hard to tell the line between land and its issue to riverbed.

Up over, though, you find the reservoir that the aqueduct feeds, throngs to: the unnatural loch, Loch Thom. It is soft rectangular dishes borne into the earth, shallow with water. Hot and dry, all the liquid only just there at the base, drawn down even from the caking sides. A kind of martian emptiness, the land quietly speaking of production.

In thin heat at the foot of the ascent. At the café, outside and right by the tables: a large tub, somewhere between a squared bathtub and a tank. You looked over its rim and it was shallow with a dark grey green slurry, water, and a kind of propeller fitted at one end of the base, rusted.

Taking a route beside the old one, where water slipped as though virtual, frictionless across a white-walled gutter _____ hard to tell if its state of half-doneness was a design feature, a gesture at indeterminacy, slightness, in the face of this coercion of liquid, OR a monument in process. The tarmac track leading up to it was freshly laid, and had this clean thickness where you got a cross section that was free yet of dust or mud from the land it inched over. Tarmacadam still pitch all over, tamped down still soft. They were welding the cattle grid at the start of the tarmac road, and passing you saw sparks.

Later, gutted slate channels. A sense of the land being scalped for its liquid.
But, despite this, it was marshy still.
lots of heathers, gorse, broom.

Earlier, in the mist, a road sign with the first word scrubbed clean off with wear, just ——— PEAT. The mist had been photographic in its sharpness. When it cleared, hours later, the taxing heat was, too.

and of course water is the master of liquid—

The wetness in the morning had been so clarifying, and the dry hot sharp clarity of midday was exactly the same. Wetness and dryness are one and the same.

what is it about this word *master* that catches so?
Is to master to control,
to keep in, a withholding,
a nonrevealing

and, if that's true, then are the *masters* of things those who you don't even know *are* those things?
Is mastering stomaching, the way glass does,
omitting interior 'true' 'essential' expression?

Is to master your essence to not let it show on your surface?
To hide your liquidity, as glass.
To take a rumbling, a gulley, a flood, and not let its effect show on your surface membrane.

Some liquid forms — and I am thinking here about a bubble, all cusp and no core — control their shape by virtue of the boundary that forms between them and all else. A bubble is a skin, the control of membrane is what it is. All cusp, no core. All a brim and all its drama in its potential, inevitable, to breach and be over.

*and of course water is the master of liquid —
but glass is not far behind*

You separate, split, go home.

II *glass*

~ You go to the corner shop for beer and they don't sell alcohol. Instead, in a panicked feeling of needing to buy something, you spend some time in the aisle, stacked full, of cleaning products. You buy a *beautiful bottle* of purple Dettol. It is purple, a soft violet, to show it doesn't smell like the *classic* brown Dettol, that it's scented with some lavender, maybe something else. The shoulders of the bottle have a seductive ebullience, a smooth roundness like a Lewis chess piece. It's this shape that first draws you to it. You buy it and some soda crystals, pay cash and leave. The soft kilo of crystals goes in the crook of your arm, the bottle firm in your right hand.

Two doors down, arm in arm with your goods, then through the front door and in. Home, you don't put the bottle in the cupboard under the sink, where all the other products stay. Instead, it goes up on a high open shelf. You think about what lines and lines of them would look like, up there. Consider a bulk order. At least as you see it from your screen, the purple's not the same as Horn's purple, the one she uses in that big weight of a glass sculpture, but it shares the calibre of it.

The sculpture atop your mind is *Untitled ("The sensation of satisfaction at having outstared a baby.")*, a broad solid cylinder of violet cast glass made by Roni Horn in 2013. It has an immediate effect of cool, cool like a lozenge. A sense of dryness on the outer edge (your tongue goes dry), where a repeat pattern of narrow vertical lines, a remnant of the twenty-four-hour casting process, embosses the surface. This is in direct contrast to the top, which, though glass too, seems more liquid, is like salivating. There is wetness here, and clearness, reflection, none of that matte edge-dry. The centre is an encircled expanse, circled by itself. On the rough side edge, there is a whiteness which reminds of brushed velvet. There's lots of texture here, difference. The reflective sups up to meet the non-reflective.

Horn pulled *The sensation of satisfaction at having outstared a baby* from a list in a short story by Hollis Frampton. Another phrase from the same list is 'a memory of the color violet, reported by those blinded in early infancy.' Maybe this is where Horn's choice in the sculpture of violet, and so violet a violet, comes from. It is a shade more memory than reality, more conceptually bound in *the past*, both in the way it is experienced as colour, and in name. It is parma violets, it is a tube of gloss for lips. AND its top is a parma violet's shape, has that concave dip on its top. On the tongue, a space of air is enclosed by that gap.

Your memory of other violets becomes it, it them. The two converse, exchange. So, the sculpture *must* be that same purple as my dettol, it could not be any other way. Your mind makes it so. You know that the sculpture is in Los Angeles, and from the website that it's not currently on view. You find yourself travelling to LA for other reasons, so try to make an appointment. Someone with a name like Wolstonecraft gets back to you, says that they're only letting staff into the vaults (your word) where the sculptures are stored. You can't do any colour matching, then. In LA everything is bleached by the sun, and it doesn't seem conceivable that such a clarified object could be existing here. A minor oasis in the dry.

In its manifestation the work underwent a twenty-four-hour pouring, then a four-month long cooling. It is as a result of this temporal elongation that the object seems as two materials, though it's just the one. The clear top surface of the work does the opposite of brim: the glass laps up to meet its side edge. An entry on wikipedia says that such a concave meniscus *occurs when the particles of the liquid are more strongly attracted to the container than to each other, causing the liquid to climb the walls of the container.* Here, glass is the container for itself, OR after the flurry of the casting process it seems so: it laps up to meet *itself* at its edge. Its surfaces are attracted to one another. Though their makeup is the same, they meet and are shown to have different qualities.

> You try to imagine
> That you could go into it
> That you could be under it
> 3300 lbs of it
> That you could even just touch it.
>
> In lieu of visiting it, you place yourself
> even closer to it.
> By vicarious weight, vicarious mass.
> A mass not permitted to be known by a flesh meeting.
>
> Arousal is lifting, upward reaching,
> as fire.
> But you feel it too when under its vertiginous opposite:
> gravity, ever drawing down, neath, under.

I disown it, [my body] *it feels good.*
                – mum on being in water, swimming.

> Back to Roni:
> *Water is lubricant to other places.*
> *It dilutes gravity when you're in it.*
> *It reduces friction when you're around it.*

This piece by Horn is the result of ingress. It is liquid glass poured into a mould. It is the entrance of soft into hard, and then a slow cooling, *a supercooling*, where the soft takes on the negative form of the hard, becomes its close opposite. Ingress by influence came too from Frampton: Horn could have been *under* his *influence*, OR *lifted* by influence, OR both. Influence can be both upward and downward reaching, can be entrance but also the will to expel, to *give form to*, outside of oneself.

So: a sculpture.
So, too: a text.

Horn understands water as *a form of perpetual relation, not so much a substance but a thing whose identity is based on its relation to other things*. I think this way about everything, need relation in order to prove myself. Anhydrogyne, then, is granted form here in glass all over seemingly solid — to gloved gallery hands, to bare fingers, to a leaf falling, to the sideways rain — but glass that is liquid nonetheless. Glass, anhydrogyne made material, is a liquid that can rest in other states, that takes a form and holds it without need of a vessel, but it is still liquid in state. It is *still* liquid. As in Horn's *Still Water*.

I think of water as a verb. I think of it as something that one experiences in its relation to other things, as opposed to in itself. Another of Horn's cast glass works, *Air Burial* (2014-17) is placed outside, on the ground in a wooded glade, up North from here in the Cairngorms. It is there in nature so that it may *adopt the identity of its surroundings*. Is that how it goes? Is the adoption of an identity reliant on context? Andrea Long Chu says gender *is something other people have to give to you*, and that *exists only in the structural generosity of strangers*. The people you have around give — gift — it to you. They, your peers, are the ones that invoke the word: they.

Of course water is the master of liquid but glass is not far behind. Might to master mean to be able to hold it in? To be able to contain oneself, to stay reserved, to present as one thing yet maintain difference within? A kind of passing? What does it mean to have a still brim, like *Untitled ("The sensation of...")*? As neither having binary gender nor a fixed material state…a passing that is emboldening, a containment that only floods for some. A flooding for a chosen person or persons or thing or things or place or places?

    A flooding is the thing that happens after a brimming.
    There needs to be a brimming.
    There needs to have been a brimming.

    A flooding is predicated on a rising
    on a brimming, on an almost-over
    on an almost-and then a yes.

    And is flooding then assent?
    Dissent and then assent?
    Disagreement: all disagreement until agreement.
    Assent as the thing after dissent.

III *gold*

~ Horn's work is never only pure formalism. No, as Félix González-Torres said in *1990: L.A., 'The Gold Field,'* Horn is aware that:

> ...the act of looking at an object, any object, is transfigured by gender, race, socio-economic class, and sexual orientation. We cannot blame them [those who think of Horn's work as formalism] for the emptiness in which they live, for they cannot see the almost perfect emotions and solutions her objects and writings give us.

Might Horn's intention, in *Untitled ("The sensation of...)*, in the making and in the extant work, have been to push forward the liquid nature of glass? To think the limits of the material, as she does in other works too. Like, in *Gold Field* (1980-82), the work that González-Torres so loved: pure gold annealed wafer thin, to the point of the release (expulsion) of one of what might have seemed its inalienable qualities — its soft durability, how it holds the shape of a bite just so. It seems to have become fragile. It's less about altering a material state, but more about revealing one: gold most malleable is shown to be all the more so.

It is a kind of freedom to extricate a quality from a material: to chomp the rain's wetness from it and access it anew, to cleave liquid's need for a vessel away from it, to run down a metal to its thinnest shave and still be able to call it object.

It is also about control.

They read that a total of around 201,296 tonnes of gold exists above ground, as of 2020: this is equal to a cube with each side measuring roughly 21.7 metres (71 ft). They read also that Horn's dad was a pawnbroker, and think about the sign of the three spheres, of a gilded Florence, of the Medicis.

Anneal all the world's gold, then. Gold, most malleable of all metals. Anneal it under pressure down to the thinness of a golden field. Take that 21.7 metre cube, (about the height of two tenements stacked atop one another) and unfurl it down, keeping one width as it is (a manageable knowable viewable limit) and then thin it away like a tongue's uncurl. Vollon's mound of butter palmed down by attention to an agile golden stream, a buttercup-telling yellow, a flashing streamer: to get a one thousand four hundred and sixty three mile-long tongue. Gleaming, moving away from you, spelling that distance, gleaming.

I look for comparison, try to envision this new golden field you have created. There are websites where you can go, input a surface area and get *half the size of this airport*, or, *about the size of Florence*, but this seems fruitless. Maybe a perimeter, a coastline, might give an idea of breadth that is something you can stomach? But, I have no urge to edge a city, to lasso some place and feel its golden width that way. I want to know how much this field of gold might light the rest, I want to know its effects on other things, I want to know how its objectness might prove itself, how it lights other bodies, how it might give *a lamp's kiss* to something else. I want to know how many of your chins it might light yellow, as buttercups.

Gold, from the Proto-Indo-European, *gelh: to shine, to gleam; to be yellow or green*. There's thought that this is about wheat, because it dries from green to golden. That chlorophyll loses its liquid, dries by having seen the sun and becomes that silvered gold: gleams by its meeting with the light, gleams by its loss of liquid, remembers the sun and shows it. This could be called transfiguration; it is a kind of alchemy. Is mastery the furthest reach or limit, as a flexing? To work, make, write, to show a new flex. *Untitled ("The sensation of satisfaction at having outstared a baby.")* shows a mastery, an embalmment, of the liquid state. *Gold Field* shows a mastery of the solid, malleability supreme.

Horn went on to make a further iteration of *Gold Field*, in the form of *Paired Gold Mats, for Ross and Felix* (1994–5), where two layers of the annealed gold were stacked, one atop the other. A field becomes a mat, the exterior interior, more intimate with a body. This sitting atop couples, they co-light the space between each other, create their own private aurora of gold (symbol: Au). Horn said of this piece to González-Torres – *there is sweat in-between*. Liquid, as sweat, ingresses, finds its way into this sculpture that bends material, OR the liquid is there already, it is present, deviant, despite, maybe even because of, two thinned planes softly resting into one another. The warm hollow of an armpit, the space between kissed palms; there is moisture there. Horn offers here *a perfect emotion, a perfect solution* (González-Torres). There is queer sweat in the gallery, and *incredible light flowing from the crumples* (Horn).

...

November.
They decide to end the bath and
take out the plug,
staying in to witness the egression.
What was an about unified mass of water ebbs,
becomes rather separate areas, softly delineated
by limbs
then more clear pools,
like the rockpools that used to form in her clavicle
under a gold loop earring
in the swimming pool in spring.

Pools of liquid define a profile of their body in the half-water.
The water tells gaps, hollows, shallows in them.
These pools are lit by low light,
it all seems calm soporific sibilant
but this is all undercut—

for — there is that irregular gurgle of the plughole!
the bath and the sink both, the toilet too!
They all fling out a gurgle, acknowledge the bath's
task of egression:
collectively felt, they each release sound.

They wait until the bath is fully empty,
until they're beginning to dry just by thin air,
then get a towel.

H once said that everything in the bathroom has the same purpose: getting rid of liquid, of waste, of water in and water out. And you agreed, have thought more about that than of anything else he ever said to you.

Late on, you find what M had mentioned back in the late Summer: that term you've been calling *anhydrogny*. You ask the library clerk at the Mitchell to help you find the book, it's not in the stacks. He asks how to spell *Horn*, then how to spell *Roni*. You speak each letter out loud. He says it's newly in, brings it over, hands it to you. You slide off the wrap sideways: it is open at the spine and the fore edge. Out come two books, the same size, one has a cover with two sideways repeated childhood photos, unmistakably Horn, while the other has two more recent images of Horn, also repeated, and in colour. You open the two in concert, a page from each at a time, alternating. Horn's doubling happens here, she repeats herself. Each book starts with three pages of paired sideways images, different between the books. Then, in one, the index begins.

The fifth entry is anhydrony:

Anhydrony is waterless water, the opposite of water. The form remains liquid, but the substance is altered — replaced with another identity. Anhydrony is dry water. Anhydrony is not a recognized word. Its nonexistence points to the difficulty of accepting its meaning.

In this word, instead of my combination *anhydrogyne*, the clinging edges of the *dro* and the *gyne* of the male and female are dropped, leaving something closer to *an-watery-roni*. *Andro* becomes just *an*, and so shifts to mean now a lack, without. *Gyny* becomes *rony/Roni*. She finds herself, edits the word to become her, nulls the binaries of it a little.

~~~
*bristling ~ the dehumidifier*

I

~ The bed heads up to the largest wall. On its verso the close, where in drowsiness, with their head so near to the wall, they hear silvering keys, the press and slacken of the yale late at night, neighbours entering, people leaving. They hear all this sharp and close. If people are smoking just in the doorway, they smell that too. Often this door is kept on the snib, and sinks inward at a touch. The valve of the building draws open, folds closed. The bedroom is an engine, it feels all this.

They too hear the rain being processed by the building, its tracing of a route chosen by gutters whose position in turn was chosen by a roofer a long while ago. The roofer's route repeats, reiterates with every rainfall. An increase: familiar temporary rivers reform and flow, progress eastward over the tarmac pavement outside. Other dissident routes are followed: the rain deviates, moths in at the unsure seal between sash window and porous sandstone. Chancing it. This ingression causes black mould, rotting on the ledge. Woodlice, spiders and nasturtium trails take this same route.

Rainfall in here is felt as though the glass of the windowpane is a cheek, a cheek that feels as flesh feels and so amplifies. We are in the mouth of the cheek's owner. It comes down melodic: a beating, a thrum, then later by many fingered tenderness. This descent of liquid and its processing by the building's gutters and the garden outside has cocooning qualities, quashes other harsher machine sounds of the street. They wake in the night to it. And, by their difference, their dryness, their warmth, they feel security. There is distinct pleasure to feeling the rain for all the qualities it possesses but its wetness. It feels like something Horn might try to do. To sever that so overbearing a part of its nature. Extricated, we derive differently, sup less dominant qualities: its strength against the window, its timbre, peppering, its scent.

In this room stands a dehumidifier. This machine collects liquid from its surrounding atmosphere. It parses airborne moisture down to fluid by condensation. This action forces dryness on a space, instigating weather in environments it occupies. I use it every day. Its solving capacities please. Its happy hum is satisfyingly productive. This pleases. To click a button in the morning and set it to action. To pass through, getting a hat, socks, some hours later, and to deem the reduction in humidity enough, and so to turn it off. A morning machine, then. This rhythm you have integrated nicely. Time passes, with each slow filling (which it does), and emptying (which I do), we play a game of time. We gulp down our own units of time that are defined by our relation, by the weather, by the temperature inside and outside: by all this room-liquid that we're collecting. I thank it for solving in part a problem.

Sometimes you forget about — and then are reminded of — its presence in the room by some means other than its sheer mass: its ambient hum, the irregular trickle, the light, the breeze, its moving fin (two static positions and one where it oscillates between them). Even if it's off, when you move it it thrums into action. Just the act of lifting spurs the dehumidifier to this activity. Contact activates it. It asks, *do you need me?*

Daily, on pressing, it consents to action, whirrs. At once it speaks numerical data on the room. A number comes up, provisional, green, on its flat face. It hazards a guess: *seventy three percent*. This number shifts over minutes as the reading becomes more accurate. This percentage is the relative humidity, *relative* because the water holding capability of the air in the room is affected by both air temperature and pressure. The warmer it is, the higher the capacity for water to be held airborne. Invariably it's cold in here, whatever the season, due to its vantage, the single glazed window, and to the fact that they need it cold to sleep. Pressing cold and humidity from the basement cavity too, is all the more pressing in this particular room. The bedroom is a diagram from school of liquid in motion.

At other times the dehumidifier evidences the moisture of the room in a more visceral way. You have to tend to it, waiting for the alert that it's full. When this happens, you slide out the water chamber from the back, evenly with a palm on either side. This action reveals the top of the chamber with its own angular handle, all white. You carry this portable element down the corridor like a milkmaid, to the bathtub in the bathroom. On the top of it there is a sticker — an arrow that suggests the point of egress, but as you tip it the water finds other routes by which to exit the vessel. You angle it to a full tip. Out water glugs, randomly, an involuntary series of sobs. The machine cries *cartesian tears* (Anne Boyer, *A Handbook of Disappointed Fate*). It sobs the bedroom liquid. This gathered water is called greywater.

*Whitewater* is what comes out the tap. *Greywater* is liquid that has been used for soft tasks: for bathing, dishwashing, rinsing, brushing teeth. Water that is flushed becomes *blackwater*. So, you might say greywater and blackwater divine activity, a living body. That the greywater from out the dehumidifier is not whitewater is a proof of something. It has undergone some change, carries dust, skin particles, spit. And as it recedes from view down the plughole it really is grey.

The liquid this dehumidifier collects is a blended slurry of: the liquid drawn up from the damp basement, its cement floor, the moist bricks down there; the liquid that rises in steam off shoulders through from a bath; sweat off sweating bodies; water from the glass on a coaster on the chest of drawers; water from coffee from the mug resting on top of the radiator, unstable; the rain off clothes from last night, piled at the foot of the bed; and moisture in the cool air through the window, infrequently opened. So, here in this room, the machine's healthy action by inference proves the bodied self. In Anaïs Nin's *Collages*, the liquid evidences of life are drawn together at the launderette. Pieces of fabric liquid off living bodies, prove living bodies by the liquid they produce:

> *Renate gathered together all the linen of the house stained with marks of love, dreams, nightmares, tears and kisses and quarrels, the mists that rise from bodies touching, the fog of breathing, the dried tears, and took it to the laundromat at the foot of the hill.*

Nin proves bodies by the evidence of embodied physical, emotional, acts. In contrast, a character in Proust's *In Search of Lost Time*, attuned to the weather, says they are *becoming an animated barometer myself*. There, the scientific, with a particularly 19th century focus on devices of measurement, rubs up against the lived world. The weather needs to be quantified by barometer in order to be real, the proof of the flesh body is not enough. The perceived friction between these: the emotive quotidian proof of the body, versus the scientific record, is of interest. I have been told this text is disembodied, OR, embodied but at an odd optic remove. It is something to do with this friction, that I am a body but a thinking one, that the text on paper is borne of a thinking living body.

In the *Phaedo*, Plato writes in the negative about the difficulty of extricating lived experience and philosophical thought. That the physical binds to thought, that you *can never get away to the unseen world* is compelling to me. I do not want to get away. The *bondage*, the soul as *always saturated with the body* seems the only truth to be sure of. A philosophy that stems from this, whether or not it is called phenomenology, is compelling. The character of Socrates in the Phaedo says the soul should attribute *no truth to anything which it views indirectly* because it's *subject to variation*. But what if indirectness is truth? OR, our only way to it.

With water, light lights it and that is what we see. Horn: *Most of what you're looking at when you look at water is light reflection.* Water can be seen then as this kind of composite, a mix of water and light: as not only water *but plus*. From Eileen Myles: *Was there ever any language to talk about the thing you wanted? Not as a woman but kind of plus, somehow.*

SO: water is seen always by inference, it is proven so. Its reflection is a part of how we understand it. You can have been bristling for a long time, sensitive to all all over, unstill water, but a *troubled surface does not reflect.* (Marguerite Yourcenar, *That Mighty Sculptor, Time*)

## II

~ It's truly winter now: there's liquid on the window panes each morning, often running to all day if the heating's not on much. You use the dehumidifier to try and capture this condensation, whose beads just seem to appear overnight. The sunlight is flagrant through them. It is as though this liquid is coming in, entering, ingressing by some nightly passage, BUT that's false. Condensation, rather, is a deviant form of ingress — in that it really isn't ingress at all. It reveals what is already present, in the same way the dehumidifier does, giving form, numerical, joined up, volume-filling liquid-taking form to something that's already extant. Like the liquid that's between Horn's two thin sheets of annealed gold, a kind of room-sweat produced by holding warm bodies close. Condensation says *I have always been here*. Contact activates it. It is the breach in temperature, the coldness out there sheer up to the warmer indoors here that causes it to come forth. Contact exacerbates this voicing of liquid: contact exacerbates this communication.

I have been bristling all over for so long because of an essential feeling of being other... This whole text is an effort in perceptual shift: in its drawing focus on ingress to the point where it's the constant out of focus presence, to where its relevance becomes implicit, to where its voice became concurrent with their thought on any subject. But, this week, it has become all too perceptive, in a very concrete way. The machine of the flat, this system of actual liquid coming in and out of here, has become self: the flat has become all a bristle to ingress. It can't get rid of the greywater. None of the drainpipes are doing their healthy job. Liquid is staying put. On the plumbers' advice sites, to paraphrase: it builds slow and then all of a sudden, mass masses in the pipes and as it gets bigger it grabs bigger bits of crud and oil and skin. It creeps up on you, and then is all at once.

Instead of its system of ingress being something implicit, it is now explicit. Nothing is draining, any tap turned on upsets the system of pipes beneath. They are interconnected down there, and this fact comes to the fore. You turn a tap on here and in the next room, at another plughole, you hear its effects: displacements of air, a blub. All of them, all the water and all the pipes, are bristling:

Bristling to watch this hand rinse.
To feel the effects of this dish wash.



I try and wash sheets and greywater lunges from the machine as I open its round door. The kitchen floor is part-cleaned by this accident, a collateral benefit. The kitchen sink is filled with a mineral caking half matte swirl — the soap from the washing machine. It takes five minutes to drain empty, and then a murmur and a white frothing up, and it fills again.

For days the sheets hang across the shower partition, dripping into the bath, OR having been handed up over the top of the kitchen door, lie wet against its faces. I turn up the heating and steam lets off them.

The plughole in the bath bristles at me, deigning to rinse a hand in the sink beside it. Its bristing is described by a guttural belly button gurg from this lowest of plugholes, the navel of the flat.

I get out the Rothenberger.

- -
- -
- -
- -

Greywater glugs out in throngs.

III

~ Eve Kosofsky Sedgwick writes that Proust's version of mysticism, which is focused on *habitual relationality, emphasises the transformative potential of the faculties of attention and perception.* You focus on the habitual, all this descriptive studding, because that is where ideas tease out. Use the daily as nourishing ground for thought, and consider what writing has to offer the daily. Cast attention to an object, a process: an observational text, like an observational drawing, is an act of care toward it. But, why this mode of approach, *this amoral, almost animal quality of attentiveness?* (Jean Acocella on Frank O'Hara). To draw meaning from the mundane as the primary source. And, too, to not use reference as a tool for getting somewhere else, or for the progression of an argument, but rather for self-positioning. This standard of attention to the quotidian is set by the title of this body of work, *ingress*. I have been bristling for a long time, and this is an experiment in bristling. In allowing such an attentive focus, a bristling towards: the word *ingress*.

To generalise: embodiment in writing presupposes an existing body, and works from that point. I feel I need to prove the existence of the body in the first place. A phenomenology via inference, imprint, reflection. An embodiment that is equally as much about attention, and being receptive to that which is outwith, as it is about the solid material body.

To write this body of work, especially the section on Roni Horn, has been largely an anguished manipulation (more than normal), of paragraphs, of quotation, of the self. Why is this? Language has always been difficult, but in the same breath the most natural medium. I think that to think about Horn is to think about gender and sexuality, and of how those always seemed so necessarily linked, and of how this was always a point of contention for me. To feel that your sexuality followed normative lines and so you couldn't solve the problem of a feeling of alterity, of queerness, via that route, and didn't yet have the language or self understanding to know yourself as non-binary. This bodily disjunct, this queerness before sexuality, to know that the site of your inner world precedes binary modes of living under gender. ... The flat is still under the pressure of a lack of egress, you've called a plumber for Friday. Dishes build, you wash your hands into a bucket and pour it out into the street.

5am, and water glugs (water-air-water-air) at the gutter by your left ear. You have been dreaming of one of those grotesquely shaped modern glass wine decanters, were thinking of it in sleep as a kind of case study. You hold its image up as though on a blackboard. Red wine fills, then empties. Now, the image is the empty vessel having been used. You think about how you'd clean it. Thin red lines show the different heights that the liquid wine met, and then retreated from; a clean run of tide lines draw a hypothetical evening. It is these lines that need washing, these evidences of liquid meeting with air. It is at these brims that the liquid makes its once-was clear. It is all in the breach! *The air as a site of alchemical state change* (Kosofsky Sedgwick again). The brim itself, and the noticing of it, as when the camellias frail en masse then drop, is the thing.

A breach is a brim is a breach is a brim.

And, it is all in the breach! The taffy pulling of time, as in Horn's slow cooling of glass, creates this breach across a single medium. That taffy pulling is anachronic, it ruptures the state of things. Deviant, glass now shows itself to be as liquid as water, it unfurls that aspect. Ingress is about difference, then: state change as much as site change.

A breach is an end: a substance that meets another substance, a quality change, a state change.

– –
– –
– –
– –
– –

I make a list every morning of what's going wrong — of things I could say. Sometimes I feel under the wave, like the subject is inevitable — like, how the visceral memory of the regular bath overflowing in the basement at Chepstow Place, and all the actions that followed: a shout, commotion, soggy towels, a bath had, were all portent to this — or were seeding it. That, what I think about regularly, the kind of things: liquid, being, ingress here, there, over there in the library, are not the stuff of other people's preoccupation. How preoccupied can one get with or by plumbing, by condensation? How rapt you be? To closely observe you also put yourself up for observation; any observation is too a reflection of the self.

A drain engineer comes, plunges twice in the kitchen and twice in the bathroom, and says the problem is fixed — but, that water is pouring directly down into the basement. Water, too, still pools in the sink. He says my fiddling with the drainhole in the bath has unlinked it to its pipe and that yesterday's bath is all over the floor down there. The next day a plumber comes and, in two minutes also, says he's fixed the problem. He goes down and tightens the pipe and that is solved. He says there's still a drainage problem, though. Together in the narrow bathroom watching the cloudy water in the sink not drain, I ask in a quiet voice if there's not anything he can do for me. He says no, I need a drainage engineer. That night I book both another plumber and another drainage engineer to come. In the morning two people turn up at the door and I ask what their specialty is. They say drainage. Quickly I know that this will be a more thorough job — they don't even bother bringing a plunger in, instead scoping out the street, looking for the point of egress there. They can't find it. One seems subservient to the other, is being told and taught things by the taller, younger man. Mainly it is this trainee who speaks to me. I tell them there's a basement and the taller one's eyes light up.

He goes down there, comes up. They go out to the van, come back with a large brushed silver drill type thing that has a big head on it like a spinning top, and a blowtorch. The main person then describes what they're going to do, to me and the trainee. They're going to cut a hole in the big cast iron pipe down there, the one that runs out onto the street (who knows where to). They'll cut a gap, enough to fit the nose of their gorgeous metallic pipe cleaner instrument. Then, solve the blockage, and then seal up the hole with a kind of bitumen tar bandage. The blowtorch then heats and sets this. He says, when the problem arises again, I can tell the drainage engineer about this bit and they can use it again as a point of access. Up in the kitchen the trainee and I can smell the tar, hear the gas flame. I run the taps and they empty fast, beautiful.

~~~
afterwards ~ the rose and the lotus

earlier:
> *Just at the window, the rain has beaded in prim rounds against the smoke tree's leaves.*

and
> *Moisture in the air beads and sags across the inside of the window panes on cold mornings.*

~ How liquid sits against that-which-it-is-not seems a preoccupation: it's evening and I'm researching how to describe the manner of contact between a liquid and a solid surface. How some liquids pool, sag to flat, and others bead. For this there is the term *wetting*, where the *wettability* of a surface is defined by the angle of contact *at which the liquid-vapour interface meets the liquid-solid interface.*

So, *perfect wetting* is an angle of contact of 0 degrees: in diagram, a flat puddle. *High wettability* is an angle between 0 and 90 degrees: in diagram, a cross section could be somewhere between a flattened pancake of a globule and a clean semicircle. Then, *low wettability* is an angle between 90 and 180 degrees, where the globule of water is a clean upright curve. Lastly, *non wetting* gives a globule that sits proud of the surface on which it rests, where the angle of contact is more than 180 degrees, and an almost full round of liquid rests against the solid. A surface, then, can in relation to water be *hydrophobic*, so *non wetting*, or *hydrophilic*, *perfectly wetting*. For other liquids, this becomes *lyophilic* or *lyophobic* — a word hard to pull into two. *Lyo* is related to dispersion, or lack of it: an affinity or a lack of affinity for another material. Arguably the two parts of both words *lyo-philic* and *lyo-phobic* contain just different shades of the same meaning. Philic as a pulling in, ingression, not being keen on dispersing, phobic as a dispersion, a repelling. The word itself is like a magnet: repellant, attracting.

I want to talk of the rose and the lotus. Of how their different surface structures mean liquid presents similarly, but acts differently on each of them: on a rose's petal, on a lotus' leaf. Both surfaces have low *wettability*, are *dewetting*, with contact angles that form droplets roundish in shape.

On a rose, *the petal effect* is evident. There's a droplet contact angle of 152.4 degrees: liquid perches in clean rounds on the surface of a rose petal. However, even though water droplets on its surface take an almost spherical shape, they cannot roll off even if the rose is turned upside-down. This is the result of the hierarchy of micro and nanostructures on each petal, which provides roughness sufficient for superhydrophobicity, creating the droplet shape, but at the same time resulting in a high adhesive force between the petal and water. Close up, where it touches, water fills all the crevices of the rough surface.

The lotus leaf has a different surface structure to the rose petal. A sufficiently rough texture means the way a droplet relates to a surface shifts from the *Wenzel* state, as in the rose (rough but with the droplet's liquid filling crevices) to the *Cassie-Baxter* state (where a droplet does not fill such crevices). In a lotus leaf, a droplet is not able to wet the microstructure space between the rough spikes on its surface, and so sits proud of this surface. This means the texture of interaction is a heterogeneous surface composed of both *air* and *solid*. Because of this lower contact area, the adhesive force between the two surfaces is very low, which allows water droplets to roll off with ease: the 'self cleaning' phenomenon.

The two materials present the same optic circumstance, that characteristic beading, but at a micro level their surface creates an opposite effect on the way droplets relate physically to them. How might these different surface qualities relate to intimacy? Others, like nasturtiums, are classic Cassie-Baxters, make contact, keep that contact angle high, come away easy. I am Wenzel all over; I allow infiltration. That capillary filling: ingress.

~~~
notes and acknowledgments

shining identification ~ not a bird, not a slug was written with edits from Jess Payn.

select anachronica – via Anaïs Nin was commissioned by Sticky Fingers Publishing as part of *Dead Lovers: Anaïs Nin* (2021). Written in conversation with and with edits from Sticky Fingers, Natascha Nanji and Evelyn Wh-ell. An excerpted version of this piece was performed at *Life's Not Personal*, a conference by Midlands4Cities/AHRC, in July 2022.

Thanks to Jill Morgan, Donna Marcus Duke, Evelyn Wh-ell, Sheran Forbes, Caitlin Merrett King, Sophie Paul, Tim Knights, Margot Wilson, Kaiya Waerea, Ben Redhead, Jess Payn, Nate Lippens, Olivia Laing, Cecilia Pavón and Richard Porter for your sensitive readings and support of the text in its various stages.

Published in the U.K. by Pilot Press

Cover Image by Kate Morgan
Design by Sheran Forbes

Copyright © Kate Morgan 2023
Copyright © Pilot Press 2023

ISBN: 978-1-7393649-1-5

All rights reserved

Printed on 100% recycled paper